TREETOPS CLA

ROBINSON CRUSOE

DANIEL DEFOE
adapted by Anthony Masters

OXFORD
UNIVERSITY PRESS

OXFORD
UNIVERSITY PRESS

Great Clarendon Street, Oxford OX2 6DP

Oxford University Press is a department of the University of Oxford.
It furthers the University's objective of excellence in research, scholarship,
and education by publishing worldwide in

Oxford   New York

Athens Auckland Bangkok Bogotá Buenos Aires Calcutta
Cape Town Chennai Dar es Salaam Delhi Florence Hong Kong Istanbul
Karachi Kuala Lumpur Madrid Melbourne Mexico City Mumbai
Nairobi Paris São Paulo Singapore Taipei Tokyo Toronto Warsaw

with associated companies in Berlin Ibadan

Oxford is a registered trade mark of Oxford University Press
in the UK and in certain other countries

ISBN 0 19 919330 4

Cover: Stock Illustration Source/John Pack
Inside illustrations: Janek Matysiak

Printed in Great Britain

About the Author

DANIEL DEFOE

1600–1731

Daniel Defoe was born in London, and was the son of a butcher. He became a merchant, travelling in Europe to sell and buy socks.

When he was 60, Defoe heard the story of a sailor called Alexander Selkirk. In 1704, Selkirk had fallen out with his ship's captain, and asked to be put ashore on an uninhabited island. Selkirk was rescued in 1709. His story gave Daniel Defoe the ideas for *Robinson Crusoe*, which was his most famous book.

After *Robinson Crusoe* was published, it was imitated by other authors, who started writing stories about shipwrecks and survival, still popular themes today.

Pronunciation note

The word 'boatswain' is pronounced <u>bo</u>-sun.

October 1st, 1659

My name is Robinson Crusoe and today I begin my journal.

I have seen my share of adventures in my time. I traded down the West coast of Africa, I was captured by pirates, spent two years as a slave to a Turkish captain, then escaped and sailed to Brazil where I set up a sugar plantation. I should have been content then, but I wasn't, and when the chance came to take part in a trading voyage to Africa, I agreed immediately. How wrong I was.

Perhaps I should have listened to my father. When I was a boy he warned me against going to sea: 'If you go, you will have time to regret it in later years, when none will be there to help you.' And it seems his warning is coming true, for now I am alone and lost.

But I mustn't despair. I have pen, paper and ink. I will try to write down the events of the coming days, so that I have some record of what has happened to me if I am rescued. And if I'm not, maybe someone will eventually find my diary and read about my life.

We ran into trouble almost as soon as we set sail for Africa. A hurricane blew our ship down the Brazilian coast for twelve days and every hour I expected her to capsize. I had never seen such a furious wind.

To our relief, the wind gradually died away – but a few hours later another storm blew up and our ship took an even greater battering.

Then, early yesterday morning, I was awoken by the voice of a lookout, crying, 'Land!' As we all ran to take a look, the deck lurched: our ship had hit a sand-bar, and was stuck fast. Mountainous waves began to wash over her. At any moment she might break up. We were terrified.

With the help of the mate we managed to launch a boat, but we had no hope of surviving in those raging seas. When we tried to row for land, the sea tossed our little boat about like a toy.

Then, to my horror, I saw a huge wave coming astern of us. A second later it capsized the boat, throwing us into the lashing foam.

Buried at first in thirty foot of water I surfaced and tried to swim. I am young and strong, and a good swimmer, but the waves which hurled me towards the land only dragged me away from it immediately afterwards.

Suddenly I felt myself dashed against a jagged rock. I reached out and clung to it. The waves tried to drag me back out to sea, but I held on until the next wave lifted me off – and threw me on to the beach of an island.

I was hardly able to believe that I had reached dry land.

To escape the crashing sea I slowly dragged myself up the cliffs. But my relief turned to despair when I checked

what I had in the way of personal possessions. All I could find was a pipe and a little tobacco in a box. I began to panic, for I was wet through, had no weapons to protect me against wild beasts, and nothing to eat or drink.

I found a fresh-water stream and drank my fill, but although I searched, there was no sign of any other survivors. At last, desperately lonely, I forced myself to look for somewhere safe to spend the night. After a long search I climbed up among the branches of a spiky tree, hoping the thorns would keep off any wild beasts.

I was so tired that I fell fast asleep.

When I woke, it was broad daylight. The weather had cleared, the sun was streaming down and the sea was calm. Best of all, the ship had lifted off the sand-bar and had been driven by the tide almost as far as the rock I had clung to yesterday.

Again I went down to the shore to look for survivors. I found three hats, one cap and two odd shoes, but that was all. It seems I am alone.

At least the ship was upright, so I decided to board her and see what I could find that would be useful. I was now starving. Food would be my first priority!

A little after noon, with the sea still flat calm, I swam out and boarded her.

Although battered, the ship hadn't broken up. If only we'd stayed on board, we'd all have been safe. The fatal mistake had been taking to the boat. Grief almost overwhelmed me when I realized this. But I had work to do.

I discovered the ship's provisions were dry, although the holds were full of water. I filled my pockets with biscuit, which I ate as I checked the rest of the stores.

I found rum, took a swig to give myself courage, and then, gathering together rope, spars and a couple of top masts, I made myself a raft. I loaded on board some sea chests which I had emptied and refilled with bread, rice,

Dutch cheeses, dried goat's flesh, corn, liquor and wine. I found some carpenter's tools – more valuable to me now than a shipload of gold. I also took pistols and muskets, powder and shot, along with a couple of rusty old swords, for I had no idea what wild beasts I might meet. I also realized I was eventually going to have to hunt for food, as the provisions I'd salvaged from the ship would not last very long.

On the way back to the island the tide was flowing so strongly that my raft ran aground and I almost lost my cargo. When at last the raft refloated, I found myself being carried into a creek by the swiftly flowing tide. Suddenly I saw a little cove and managed to steer towards it, though I almost lost my precious cargo again. Finally, and with great difficulty, I landed.

My next job was to take a look at the island itself. About a mile away there was a steeply rising hill and beyond that, a ridge of more hills. Taking one of my weapons with me, I struggled to the top – only to find I was looking down at an ocean which stretched as far as the eye could see. There were rocks some way out and two small islands about three leagues to the west, but that was all.

The island I am on is barren and seems uninhabited except by wild beasts. I shot a great bird – it turned out to be a hawk – but its flesh was unfit to eat. I believe the sound of the shot was the first ever heard on the island, for as soon as I fired, a confused screaming rose from all parts of the wood and I realized the dense trees hid all kinds of birds and beasts. But no humans.

I am alone on the island, with no idea of when rescue will come – if it ever does.

October 24th, 1659

On the days that followed my arrival, I kept paddling my raft back to the ship, returning with all kinds of useful goods. These included more tools, building materials, more muskets and ammunition as well as hammocks and bedding. I even took the sails and rigging. In fact I salvaged so much that I had to make a second raft to carry it all. I also decided to rescue the ship's dog and cats. At last I had some companionship, for the grateful dog, delighted to be free at last, bounded round the island, but always returned to my side.

The rain has fallen steadily, and although sometimes the sun shines I have come to the conclusion that I have been shipwrecked during the rainy season.

To keep the rain off, I made a small tent from a sail and poles I had found. I piled all the empty chests and casks in a circle round the tent as fortifications, and blocked up the doorway with boards – all of which I'd salvaged from the ship. When I sleep at night I lie with two pistols by my head and a rifle beside me. I am ready to defend myself.

I've now made eleven voyages to and from the ship. On the twelfth day the wind began to rise and I made my last voyage, for the sea was becoming too rough for me to approach her. I discovered some more tools and a lot of money – pieces of eight, gold and silver.

But what do I need money for?

October 31st, 1659

A good discovery: there are wild goats on the island, and I have killed and eaten two.

November 4th, 1659

It has rained without ceasing for many days, with great gusts of wind. As a result of the gale, the ship has broken up and now I can only see her wreck at low water. For the past week, I have spent the daylight hours covering up all the supplies I rescued, keeping them as dry as I could.

The loss of the ship was like the loss of an old friend and my last remaining link with civilization. I grew very depressed, but I have now decided to draw up a list of good and bad points about my situation.

BAD	GOOD
I am shipwrecked on a desolate island.	I am alive.
I am alone.	I was saved while others drowned.
There seems little chance of rescue.	I have food and drink and shelter, and I rescued many useful things before the ship went down.
I don't have any clothes.	The climate is warm.
The ammunition will run out and I will have no defence.	There seem to be no wild beasts that will attack me.

Although I have seen no wild beasts on this island, I am sometimes troubled by memories of those I have seen in the past. On my voyage around Africa, I saw lions and other cruel wild animals which devoured men without mercy. I would feel safer here if I had some protection against whatever creatures may live here. So, thinking ahead to the future, I have decided to build a fortified camp. A few days ago, I found a small clearing on the side of a hill with a shallow cave. If I build my camp here, I will have shelter from the sun, and will be able to see what is happening above and below me.

I have pitched my tent in front of the cave. Around it, I plan to drive in two rows of stakes in a half circle. Then I will cut up some old wine casks and tie them between the stakes until I have a strong fence. I will also make a short ladder to go over the top of the fence. Finally, I will make a larger, stronger tent out of sailcloth to protect me from the rain.

November 5th, 1659

This morning I went hunting in the woods with my dog and killed a wildcat. Her skin is pretty and soft, but her flesh is uneatable. I take the skins from every creature I kill and preserve them, so that eventually I will be able to make some clothes. Those I have saved from the ship will not last for ever.

November 12th, 1659

I have succeeded in making a table and a chair. It was hard and difficult work, unlike anything I've ever done before, but eventually I've made something I can sit on and something I can sit at, even if they both wobble. Slowly I'm beginning to feel a little more civilized, as if I might have a chance of surviving as an intelligent man rather than a wild animal. I salvaged a few books from the ship before it sank, mainly Bibles and prayer books, so at least I have some reading material.

November 18th, 1659

I've begun to widen and deepen the shallow cave in the hillside to make more room for my possessions. For this work I have made a spade from some hard wood, and also a basket to carry out the earth I dig.

Every morning I go for a walk with my dog and my gun and we never fail to bring back something to eat. Life is getting better – if it weren't for the loneliness. The lack of any human voice except for my own is almost impossible to bear.

November 20th, 1659

My work on the cave has given me another idea. It is a

great struggle to lift the baskets of earth over the fence around my tent, so I am using the earth to strengthen the fence itself.

Each time I come out of the cave with a full basket, I go to the fence and pile the earth against it. In this way I am slowly turning the fence into a strong wall, which should well withstand any storms like the one which shipwrecked me here.

December 10th, 1659

For the last few weeks I've been working hard on widening and lengthening my cave. I want to make it big enough to accommodate a store, kitchen, dining-room and cellar.

While I was doing this I stayed in my tent, but sometimes the rain came down so hard that even the tent couldn't keep me dry. After one night when I got completely soaked, I covered the entire area with long poles from rock to rock, and thatched them with large leaves to create one enormous bivouac.

I was just thinking that my cave was almost finished when a huge quantity of earth fell on me and I was almost buried alive. Because of this I will have to renew the whole structure, scraping out the loose earth and carrying it outside and then using props to make sure the ceiling doesn't fall in again.

December 27th, 1659

This afternoon I killed a young goat and injured another.
I caught the wounded animal and carried it home.

Back at my camp, I made a splint to put on the goat's
broken leg. I had to knock the creature out to stop it
struggling while I fitted the splint, but it soon recovered.

January 26th, 1660

I have taken great care of my injured goat and now it has recovered.

To my surprise, however, although the little creature could easily run away, it has become so tame that it feeds on the grass nearby and refuses to leave me. This has given me the idea of breeding goats so that I don't have to hunt for food.

April 16th, 1660

Yesterday I finished the wall. It is very thick and strong and I have finally persuaded myself that if anyone comes from the shore, my camp will be perfectly disguised.

But today, disaster struck again. Suddenly the earth came crumbling down from the roof of my cave, and two of the posts that were propping up the roof cracked in the most terrifying manner.

I ran out of the cave, climbed up the ladder and scrambled over the wall. Rocks were falling from the hillside around me, and below me the waves crashed on the beach with tremendous force.

I was in the middle of an earthquake.

Suddenly I looked up and saw a chunk of rock tumbling down the hillside towards me. I threw myself to one side only just in time.

After a while I could feel no more shocks and I sat on the ground in a daze. Gradually the sky became overcast and the wind began to rise. In less than half an hour the most dreadful hurricane broke out, far worse than the storm that had wrecked my ship. The sea was covered with foam and froth, the shore was flooded and trees were torn up by their roots.

The hurricane lasted for about three hours and I sat and watched its tremendous force, knowing that I was far safer outside than I was in my cave or anywhere near the trees or rocks.

At last the wind began to blow itself out and the sea became calm again. Then the rain came down and I felt it was safe enough for me to go back into my cave.

June 16th, 1660

Going down to the beach today I found a large turtle. It was the first time I had seen such a creature on the island. I killed the thing and spent a long time cooking her over my fire. I also found three score eggs inside her. Her flesh is the most savoury and succulent that I have ever tasted in my life.

June 25th, 1660

Whether it was the earthquake, the hurricane, the

perpetual rain or the turtle I've no idea, but I soon found myself feeling sick and shivering violently.

On June 20th I lay awake all night, feverish and with violent pains in my head. Was I dying? I had no medicines to dose myself with, and being ill so far from civilization terrified me. I prayed to God to help me, although I was so sick and confused I hardly knew what I was saying.

For the next three days I lay desperately ill.

The fever has passed now, but it has made me realize how truly alone I am here.

June 26th, 1660

I was feeling a little better this morning so I took myself off with my dog and my gun, hoping to hunt. I found myself so weak, however, that I could barely walk. I forced myself on and managed to kill a she-goat, but I hardly had the strength to carry her home – as I now thought of my camp.

Once back in the cave I cooked some of the goat and ate it slowly. I wish I could have stewed the thing and made some broth, but I have no pot.

June 28th, 1660

Yesterday I fell ill again and lay in bed all day in despair, neither eating nor drinking. Then, last night, I had the most dreadful dream. I imagined I was sitting on my wall, when I saw a man of fire descend from a great black cloud and stand on the grass in front of me. I couldn't bear to look at him because his body was so bright. His face was a terrible sight – so terrible that I can't describe it – and when he strode upon the ground the earth shook as if he was the very spirit of the earthquake itself.

The ghostly figure began to walk towards me with a long spear in his hand and I realized he was going to kill me.

Then he shouted, 'Seeing all these things hath not brought thee to repentance, now thou shalt die.'

As he spoke these words my terrifying visitor lifted his spear, pointed it at my heart – and disappeared from sight in a massive sheet of flame.

It was only a nightmare, but that did not stop me thinking about it afterwards.

It is true I have not been a good man – some would say I've had a mis-spent life. Suddenly I began to wonder if being shipwrecked on this island is my punishment for some of the things I've done. Was I condemned, then, to spend the rest of my life here? The thought plunged me into despair.

Then, for some reason, I remembered the Bible I had saved from the ship. When I opened it, my eyes fell on the words, 'Call on me in the day of trouble, and I will deliver thee.' Suddenly I seemed to see an answer. Perhaps being shipwrecked here is a punishment – but I have been spared from death for a reason. There is hope, if I can put my trust in God. From now on, I will try to be a better man.

July 15th, 1660

At last I feel stronger and it looks as if I'm really getting better. Maybe the island gave me the illness so I could build up resistance to the tropical diseases that must abound here. Was that a God-given gift? I'm alone, battling against the elements, and I have to be grateful for *anything* I'm given.

Today, I decided I had to explore. I have no real idea of how big the island is. If I do a survey, I might, after all, find something to my advantage. Possibly even another human being. Or is that just a fantasy?

I set off up the creek where I had first brought my rafts ashore. After two miles I discovered the tide didn't flow any higher and the creek became no more than a little brook. The water was fresh and cool and simply marvellous to drink.

Meadows surrounded my little stream, and I found not only tobacco plants but also several sugar canes. There were other fruits and plants too, but I couldn't identify them, so I have no idea whether they are poisonous or not. I have named the place 'The Valley of Plenty'.

July 16th, 1660

Today, as I continued to explore, I found the countryside became much more wooded and I came across fruit I could recognize, such as clusters of grapes, and melons. Further on there were cocoa trees, orange and lemon and other citrus trees, and green limes whose juice I mixed with water. I have laid up a store of fruit which will help me through the rainy season – I have brought home all I could carry, and will return for the rest. I will try to dry the grapes, to make raisins.

I walked home feeling much more cheerful. This would be a good place to live. I will spend more time there, and see if I like it.

August 3rd, 1660

I have decided to pitch a tent down in the Valley of Plenty, and build a fence around it. Although there is less shelter here than in my original camp on the hillside, the land is fertile and I am easily able to find food. I will call this my 'Country Estate'.

August 14th, 1660

It has begun to rain again, so I will return to my original camp.

September 20th, 1660

I'm surprised by the sudden increase in my family of cats. One of them had run away and I had feared she was dead, but eventually, around the end of August, she returned home with three kittens at her side.

The wildcat I had killed with my gun was very different from the cats found in Europe, but although the ship's cat must have mated with one of the wildcats her kittens seemed to me to look exactly the same as the ones I'd been used to. Soon the same happened with my other cat, who was also female. Before long I may be pestered by dozens of kittens!

The rain has been lashing down continuously since the middle of August, and I have hardly stirred out of the cave. I went out twice and came back soaked to the skin, but at least with food. My menu is now becoming less boring, particularly after I found another turtle. Today, for example, I ate some raisins for my breakfast (a bunch of grapes that I had dried), a piece of goat and some turtle flesh for my lunch and a few turtle eggs for supper.

September 30th, 1660

I have now come to the anniversary of my shipwreck and my landing on the island. I'd been keeping a check on the days by making notches on a cross, and they now amount to three hundred and sixty-five days.

I knelt down, thanking God for his mercy, and to show my gratitude I fasted for over twelve hours, not touching a morsel of food or taking one drop to drink. I then ate some biscuit and some fresh grapes, and went to bed.

October 3rd, 1660

This evening I have had to accept that my ink is running out. I have therefore decided to use it more sparingly and to write down only the most important events of my life from now on.

November 15th, 1660

This morning I sowed some grain. I only have a little, so I decided not to risk all of my store. Only time will tell whether it succeeds.

November 25th, 1660

Today I returned to inspect my Country Estate. It was still intact, although I had some difficulty finding it, because of a surprising change. Where I expected to find my home, all I could see was a clump of young trees. On closer inspection, these proved to be the stakes I had cut to make the fence. They had sprouted long branches and grown taller, taking on a life of their own. In fact they have become young trees and I am delighted by their sturdy growth. I will make a similar fence around my original camp, as it will then be perfectly disguised.

I now understand that the seasons of the year on the island can't be divided into spring, summer, autumn and winter, but into rainy seasons and dry seasons. This is how they work out:

Half February ⎫
March   ⎬ Rainy
Half April   ⎭

Half April		
May		
June	}	Dry
July		
Half August		

Half August		
September	}	Rainy
Half October		

Half October		
November		
December	}	Dry
January		
Half February		

April 29th, 1661

I have harvested my first crop of grain! The crop I sowed back in November failed, but another crop sown in March of this year has sprouted and grown! I may even be able to make bread . . .

July 2nd, 1661

I've been dividing my time between my original camp on the hillside and my Country Home. There was much work to be done in both places, and I have been busy making repairs and extensions.

I then decided to travel across the island and make a thorough exploration. Taking my gun, a hatchet, a large quantity of powder and shot and as much biscuit, cake and raisins as I could carry, I finally set out one morning with my faithful dog.

As I walked I tried to work out where my island is. On a clear day I can see land to the west, at least twenty leagues away. If this land was that part of the American coast occupied by Spain, I would have seen ships passing, so it is much more likely to lie between the Spanish colonies and Brazil. This has always worried me. I know for a fact that the very worst savages live here. They are cannibals, and never fail to murder and eat any humans who fall into their hands.

The other side of the island is much more attractive than mine. There are open fields with flowers and grass, beautiful woodland, and a large number of parrots. I decided to try to capture one, tame it and teach it to speak to me. The bird wouldn't have a human voice, but at least it would be company, for I am so unbearably lonely. Eventually I managed to knock a parrot out of a tree with a stick. Fortunately the bird quickly recovered and I took it with me on my journey.

Further on, there were hares and foxes, rather different

N

Secret
Beach

North-South
Ridge

Country
Estate

Grassy Meadow

Lookout
Rock

Sea Coast
Home

Calendar
Cross

Shipwreck
Rocks

31

from the ones I was used to at home but recognizable none the less.

At last I came to the opposite seashore. The coastline here is much more attractive than on my side of the island. More important to me, this shore was covered with hundreds of turtles, whereas I considered myself lucky if I found one or two on mine.

I travelled along the coast for about twelve miles and then, having set up a huge pole on the shore as a marker, I decided to go home again, but taking a different route.

In fact this was to prove too difficult, because the weather grew so misty I couldn't see the sun and therefore couldn't navigate. I found myself in a large valley that was surrounded by hills covered in woodland. I had no idea which direction to take so I retraced my steps to my marker and returned home the way I had come. By the time I got home, I was exhausted.

August 28th, 1661

The rainy season has arrived, forcing me to pass more time in the shelter of my home. I have spent the days teaching my parrot, whom I've named Poll, to talk and, above all, say my name.

I would not say that I am happy here – I still dream of being rescued – but I have accepted that my fate, for

now, is to stay on this island. I am living a better life here than I did in the old days, before I was shipwrecked.

September 30th, 1662

I have now been on the island for almost three years.

I have not been idle in the past few months. My corn has had to be protected from goats, hares and birds. Then I needed to learn how to make bread – though I have no grindstone to grind the corn, and no yeast. At first I tried to make a grindstone out of rock, but this was too soft; instead I used a hard wood, and this has worked well. The yeast I have had to do without. But I have also succeeded in making clay pots to bake my bread in. They are mis-shapen, ugly things, but they work. I shaped them out of raw clay, let them dry in the sun, then 'fired' them in a bonfire. I even managed to make a pot which could hold liquid; one of my pots became coated in sand before I fired it, and when I took the pot out of the fire, I discovered that the sand had melted into a glaze!

It has taken months to achieve all this – but today I sampled my first small barley loaves.

January 5th, 1663

Some months ago I decided to make a canoe. I cannot count on its being a means of escape because of the

hundreds of miles of uncharted waters around the island – and if I try to reach the nearby land I run the risk of meeting cannibals! But at least I could explore the coast, which would make me feel less trapped on the island.

I chose a vast cedar tree in the woods. I spent twenty days chopping it down, and a further fourteen days hacking off the branches. A month passed while I shaped the tree into a boat and it took nearly three months while I hacked out the inside. Eventually I succeeded in making a huge canoe with more than enough space for myself and my cargo.

But I deliberately pushed one problem to the back of my mind – how to get such a large, heavy boat into the water. The craft lies about a hundred yards from the sea and it is too heavy for me to drag any distance. All my work has been wasted.

March 8th, 1664

I have decided to make another canoe. My heart is sick at the thought of all the work this will mean. But I must not allow myself to be defeated by setbacks.

This time I will make a smaller one, and think carefully about where I build it, so that I have a chance of floating it when it is finished!

June 19th, 1665

My canoe is finished and launched!

Even though I tried to make the job of launching it easier for myself, I found I still had to dig a canal from my 'boatyard' to the creek, so that I could float the canoe at high tide. Just digging the canal has taken me months. But I have succeeded!

That moment of triumph, when I brought the canoe through the canal to the creek, was the greatest joy I have ever felt in my life.

I then fixed up a small mast and sail. Finally, I made lockers at either end of the canoe so that I could stow provisions as well as ammunition. I also cut into the side of the craft so that I could place my gun in the hollow, making a flap to hang over the weapon to keep it dry. If I meet any enemies on the sea, I shall be able to defend myself.

November 6th, 1665

At last I am nearly ready to set sail.

Today, I fixed an umbrella I had made in a step in the stern to keep the worst of the sun off my head. I then loaded my lockers with two dozen loaves of bread, a pot of rice, a small bottle of rum, half a goat and powder and shot. I also have on board two large, heavy coats I salvaged from the wreck; I will lie on one and use the other to cover me up at night.

December 23rd, 1665

My voyage around the island took me much longer than I had thought. About two leagues out to sea, there were a large number of rocks, some above water and some underneath, and beyond the rocks was a shoal of sand. I realized I would have to take my canoe a long way out to sea, go right round them and then find somewhere where I could land again.

The thought of sailing so far from the island worried me, so I went ashore and climbed a hill to get my bearings. From the hill I could see that a very strong current ran to the east and even came close to where I had landed. I soon realized that if I wasn't careful, the current could sweep me so far out to sea that I wouldn't be able to get back to the island that I now called home.

I stayed ashore for a couple of days, as the wind was blowing strongly from the south-southeast. On the third day it dropped and I set off in my canoe again. But however hard I tried to avoid the current, I was still caught by its fearsome pull. It dragged the canoe onward with terrifying violence. There was no wind to help me and the paddle was useless.

Then I saw something ahead which made me despair. The current ran on *both* sides of the island. In a few leagues the two fierce currents would join. All I had feared was coming true. I couldn't get home. I would circle the island in the current for the rest of my days.

Using the paddle and utterly exhausting myself, I kept the canoe as much to the north as possible so that I could take advantage of an eddy towards the side of the current.

Suddenly I felt a breeze on my face and I was a little more cheered.

Half an hour later, the breeze became a strong wind. I spread my sail and the wind and current carried me back towards the island, to the 'home' I had believed I was never going to see again.

When I got back on shore I fell to my knees and thanked God for my deliverance.

After a long sleep on the beach, I returned to my country house in the Valley of Plenty. I climbed over the fence, lay down in the shade and slept yet again – until I heard a voice calling my name.

'Robin. Robin. Robin Crusoe. Poor Robin Crusoe. Where are you, Robinson Crusoe? Where are you? Where have you been?'

At first I was terrified. Then I saw my dear Poll. He was simply repeating the words I had taught him, but it sounded as if he was overjoyed to see me and I was greatly moved.

January 6th, 1677

The years seem to have passed at an incredible speed. My dog, and the cats I first brought to the island, are now dead. I have improved my two homes, grown crops and made bread, milked my increasing herd of goats and trapped wild animals for food and for their skins. I have made myself clothes from those skins: I have a cap made of goatskin with a flap behind, to keep the sun off, and a goatskin jacket and breaches. I have no shoes or stockings, but I have made myself rough boots from skins, which I tie around my legs. From my goatskin belt I carry a saw on one side and a hatchet on the other; I've also got pouches for powder and shot for my guns. As I go about the island I carry a basket on my back and a gun at my shoulder.

What a sight I must be – but for years I believed that no one would ever see me like this. Until yesterday.

I was walking over the beach to the canoe about noon, when I saw the print of a man's naked foot in the sand.

I stood there as if I had been struck, not able to move. I listened for a human voice above the familiar sounds of the waves and the seabirds, but though I strained my ears I could hear no one. And yet the footprint was fresh and clear.

Then I began to wonder if I had got confused and was staring down at my own footprint, forgetting that I had already passed that way. Was this a possibility? I took off my goatskin boot and set my foot down beside the footprint. The foot which had made it was clearly bigger than my own. Someone else has been on the island.

I returned home terrified, glancing behind me time after time, seeing human shapes behind every tree.

I reached my camp, went like a fox to earth and didn't sleep all night. Who could the footprint belong to? Who was trespassing on my island? A cannibal? Or the devil himself? I held the Bible close to my chest and waited for the dawn.

Today, I have begun to fortify my hillside home, including both cave and camp. I have also made musket holes in the wall surrounding my home, so that I can fire at approaching enemies.

43

January 19th, 1679

Four days ago – two years after I saw the footprint – I thought I saw a boat out to sea at a great distance.

When I reached the shore at the far end of the island I saw a sight that utterly horrified me and made me far more fearful than the footprint had.

The beach was covered with bones and skulls, lying bleached white on the sand, and in the centre was a place where a fire had been lit. I realized I was gazing at the remains of a cannibal feast. I had been on the island for nineteen years and never seen anything like this before. I felt sick.

I had never explored this part of the island before and I began to wonder if the cannibals had regularly enjoyed their gruesome picnic on this beach. Perhaps they came often. Perhaps I was just lucky to have been cast ashore on the side of the island they did not visit. But what if they should one day come to my part of the island?

I hurriedly returned to my camp and checked my weapons. I had three pistols, two muskets and plenty of ammunition, as well as the two rusty swords I'd rescued from the ship. If the cannibals explored the rest of the island and decided to attack me, at least I'd be ready for them.

Each day since then I've climbed to the top of the hill so that I can watch for boats, but I've seen none. Even so, I was afraid that the smoke rising from my fire might be

seen. But I knew I couldn't survive without baking bread and cooking meat. Then I had a brainwave. I burnt some wood under turf, as I'd seen it done in England, until it became charcoal. Then I put the fire out and used the hot charcoal to cook with instead. Now there was no more smoke.

January 22nd, 1679

This morning I had another bad shock. I was cutting down a small tree when I found a large hollow behind a pile of brushwood.

I stared into the shallow cave and saw two broad, shiny eyes gazing steadily back at me. What creature could this be? A cannibal hiding so close to my home, waiting to attack me? I muttered a quick prayer. Then, gathering my courage, I picked up a blazing stick and rushed in – only to hear a sigh that put me into a cold sweat. For a moment I was too terrified to move, but I forced myself on – and saw, lying on the ground, a huge he-goat, gasping for breath and dying of what I'm sure was old age!

December 9th, 1682

I have been on the island now for over 23 years. I would be happy here, but for the fear of the cannibals – though almost three years have passed since I saw the boat. Even so I have been careful to keep guns about me, to watch out for boats and to make sure I did nothing which would draw attention to me. For a whole year I even avoided chopping wood and making things, in case the noise gave away my presence. Gradually, however, the fear passed, though I always kept my guns ready. I am glad now that I did.

I was harvesting my crops yesterday when I saw the light of a fire on *my* side of the island, only a couple of miles away.

I went straight to my hillside camp, knowing that if anyone found my excellent crop of corn they would soon realize someone was living here. I pulled up the ladder, loaded my weapons and began to pray to God for deliverance.

But after a while I knew I couldn't bear sitting here any longer without knowing what was going on. Cautiously, I clambered to the top of the hill. There I perched behind a rock, trusting that this would shelter me from view.

Using my perspective glass, a nautical magnifier I had rescued from the wreck years ago, I made out nine naked

Indians sitting around a fire on the beach. They had two canoes with them which they had hauled up on to the sand.

Later, when the tide had turned, they put out to sea again. I went to another vantage point. From there I spotted *five* canoes out at sea – the other three must have landed on another beach. I also noticed more bones and uneaten parts of human bodies on the beach. There was blood everywhere, staining the golden sand.

May 17th, 1684

I haven't seen any sign of the Indians for over a year, but I've been in constant fear of them returning and taking me by surprise. I've been sleeping badly, dreaming terrible dreams. Then, last night, I had another sign that I am not as alone as I thought.

A gale blew all yesterday, with a good deal of thunder and lightning. I woke from a troubled sleep, fancying I'd heard the sound of a gun being fired out at sea.

Racing to the top of the hill I saw a flash of fire and heard a second shot. I wondered if it might be a ship in distress. Dragging together all the dry wood I could find, I set my bonfire ablaze to guide any boats towards my island. The wind was so fierce that the fire soon died out, but when I heard another gunshot, I built up the fire again and worked even harder to keep it alight.

49

But when dawn came I could see only the wreck of a ship on the rocks.

Still, there might be survivors. The sea was much calmer now. Surely I could risk a voyage in my canoe? But when, paddling hard, I approached the worst of the currents, I hesitated. Despite my desire to help any survivors – despite my terrible need to see a human face – I knew I was heading for danger again. I remembered the horror of those currents, and how I thought I'd never get back home again.

I paddled my canoe up a little creek and sat on the shore, trying to work out which currents would safely take me to the wreck and then return me to the island. I finally decided to keep to the north.

After sleeping the night in the canoe I returned to the sea, and in less than two hours I had reached the wreck.

The ship had stuck fast, jammed in between two rocks. The waves were gradually breaking her up. Was there no one left alive? But as I hove close to, a dog ran out on her deck, yelping and crying. When I called to him he jumped into the sea, swimming to my canoe, and I hauled him aboard.

The poor creature was almost dead from hunger and thirst. I gave him bread and water, and he ate like a ravening wolf. It was a joy to care for him.

I then went on board.

The first sight I saw was two members of the crew who had drowned in the galley. They had their arms around each other.

Water had penetrated everywhere and the provisions were ruined. All I could salvage was a small cask of brandy, several muskets and powder, a fire shovel and tongs, two brass kettles and a copper pot. There were also various chests. At first I thought they contained only some clothes, but hidden among them I later found three great bags of pieces of eight, six gold doubloons and some small gold bars. Yet I value them less than the dog who is my new companion.

May 10th, 1685

I have kept constant watch for the cannibals, and today they returned: this morning I discovered no less than five canoes pulled up on the shore on my side of the island! There was no sign of their occupants.

I clambered up to the top of the hill, taking care that my head didn't show: I was sure that if they discovered me, I couldn't take on so many. With the help of my perspective glass I saw there were about thirty Indians and that they had lit a fire and were preparing to roast meat. I wondered if the meat was human.

I got my answer soon enough. As I watched, the Indians returned to their canoes and dragged out two men. One of them was immediately knocked unconscious. As I watched in horror, the Indians began to carve up his body, cutting him up in pieces for cooking.

While they did this, they left the other victim standing by himself, ready to be hacked to pieces. Perhaps they thought he wouldn't dare try to escape. But suddenly he started to run with incredible speed along the sands towards me.

Three of the cannibals immediately took up the chase.

He swam the creek that lay between his pursuers and my cave, despite the fact that the tide was high – he must have been an extremely powerful swimmer. Only two of the Indians could swim. The other paused by the bank and then ran back to his fellow cannibals.

I suddenly realized that I had to save this man's life.

I raced down my ladder, grabbed my guns, took a short cut through the trees and sprinted towards him. 'Follow me!' I shouted to him. Of course, he didn't understand; instead he seemed terrified.

Then I rushed at the two Indians. The first I knocked down with the stock of my musket – I didn't want to fire in case it brought the others over the river towards me. But his companion aimed a bow and arrow at me, and I was forced to shoot him in the head.

At the sound, the Indians on the beach looked towards

us. Would they follow? But the noise seemed to fill them with fear: they fled to their boats and immediately began paddling furiously. Clearly they had never heard the sound of gunfire before.

I turned back to the Indian I had rescued. He stood stock-still, staring down at his two fallen enemies, too frightened to move. When I signalled him to approach me, he trembled as if *he* had been taken prisoner and was about to be killed.

Slowly, however, he walked towards me – then he knelt down before me, kissed the ground and, taking my foot, set it on his head. I took this to mean that he was promising to be my slave.

But I had only stunned the first Indian with the butt of my musket. Just then he began to come round. My new friend glanced at my sword and signalled to me that he needed it. I handed it to him, and he slowly walked over to his enemy, and with one blow, cut off his head.

Together, we buried the bodies; then I took my new friend back to my cave, where I gave him bread, a bunch of raisins and some water to drink. When we had eaten, I made signs for the man to lie down and go to sleep, pointing to a place where I had laid a heap of straw and where there was a pile of blankets.

I have decided to call him Friday, for the simple reason that today is Friday. He is a tall, handsome fellow and is probably about twenty-six years old, with long black hair, a high forehead and a round, plump face.

After all these long years of loneliness, I am overjoyed to have a companion at last.

May 11th, 1685

Friday does not seem to understand that I am completely against the eating of human flesh, for today he took me back to the place on the beach where we had buried his enemies, and indicated that we should dig them up and eat their flesh. I tried to express my anger and outrage at the idea and I believe he soon began to realize that cannibalism was *not* something that he and I were going to enjoy together.

Taking a sword and guns, and with Friday's bow and arrow, we went back to the shore where the cannibals had been. The sand was covered with human remains. Using sign language, Friday made me understand that there had been a great battle amongst rival tribes; prisoners had been taken, and the victors planned to celebrate with a cannibal feast.

I asked Friday to clear up the remains and made a great fire on the sand to burn them. As he worked I could see that he hankered after the flesh and was still a cannibal at heart. I hope I will be able to lead him into better ways.

May 28th, 1685

I have begun to teach Friday a few words of English, and as the days pass I have begun to realize that no man could be a more faithful friend than Friday, although our relationship is more like father and son.

To help Friday lose his taste for human flesh, I decided to offer him other kinds of meat and took him into the woods to kill a young goat. It was also a good opportunity to show him how a gun worked, as this was still a complete mystery to him.

I have also given him some clothes to wear – he found them strange at first, but I think he is rather proud of them now.

September 2nd, 1685

After a few months, Friday's English is improving, and I have been able to ask him how he came to be taken prisoner by the enemy tribe. He told me that his tribe was the stronger, but that the group of warriors he was with had been outnumbered by the enemy.

'But why didn't your people rescue you?' I asked.

Friday explained that he had been taken away by canoe. 'My tribe have no canoe that time,' he said.

'What does your nation do with the men *they* take?' I asked. 'Do they eat them as these did?'

'Yes, my nation eat mans too, eat all up,' Friday explained. 'They come here.'

'Have you been here with them?'

'Yes, I been here.' And he pointed to the northwest side of the island, which, it seems, was where his tribe held their feasts.

I also learned from Friday that the currents around this island change between morning and afternoon. If I had picked a different time to try my canoe, I might not have had such a desperate journey. Perhaps, with his help, I may one day be able to escape.

In return, I have told Friday my own story; he seems able to understand most of what I say. I have taught him to shoot. I have described the countries of Europe to him and, in doing so, made myself even more homesick than before. I have also shown him what is left of my ship – which is very little after so many years. When he understood that I had arrived on the ship he said something that at first I didn't understand.

'Me see boat like this come to place at my tribe.'

Eventually I realized he meant that another ship had been driven up on the shores of his island and that his people had saved the white men from the sea. What was even more interesting was that they hadn't killed and eaten them – they only ate men who came to fight against them – and that the seventeen survivors still lived amongst the tribe.

December 4th, 1685

I was standing with Friday on top of the hill on a very clear day when he became excited, pointing to the distant land on the horizon. This, he said, was his home. I wondered whether he was homesick, so I asked him about his future, for I didn't want to keep Friday if he was miserable.

Did he really want to go home? He said yes, but he couldn't swim that far, and when I said I'd make him a canoe he replied that he would only return to his island if I agreed to go with him. Hoping there could still be white men on the island I agreed. Soon we began to make plans.

February 6th, 1686

It's the rainy season again. My canoe is too small to take both of us, so Friday and I have built a large canoe and I have managed to fit our craft up with mast and sails. When I thought of how long I took to build my first canoe, I was amazed how much faster the job has been with both of us working together.

To protect our new canoe during the torrential rain, we brought her up the creek. Friday made a small dock at high water that was just big enough to hold her, and just deep enough to keep the canoe afloat. When the tide was out we made a dam at the end of the dock to keep the sea out, and built a thatched canopy over the boat. It must be kept safe if we are to escape from the island.

April 17th, 1686

The rainy season has passed. This morning, as we were about to set off on our voyage, I asked Friday if he would go down to the shore and try to find us a turtle to eat on the journey. But he soon came running back in a terrified state, saying he'd seen three canoes heading for our shores.

The cannibals were back.

'Don't worry,' I said. 'We have enough guns and ammunition to fight them.' I hoped it was true.

To keep our spirits up, we both had a dram of the precious rum that I had kept for so many years. I felt much the better for it. I think Friday did too. I then taught Friday how to load two shotguns with large shot. I myself loaded four muskets and a couple of pistols. I took a sword and Friday armed himself with his hatchet. We were ready for them.

Taking my perspective glass we climbed the hill. From there I could see that twenty-one cannibals, three prisoners and three canoes were up on the beach. A large banquet was being prepared. The cannibals had landed much nearer to my creek this time, where a thick wood came close down to the sea.

I divided up the weapons between us and put a small bottle of rum in my pocket. Then we set out for the battle.

We entered the wood and crept down towards the beach, keeping well out of sight. Using a small thicket as cover, we approached the cannibals who were sitting round the fire, eating the flesh of one of their prisoners.

Friday went to check the numbers again. He returned with news. The Indians were not of his tribe. But more important: one of the prisoners was a white man, a Spaniard from the shipwreck he had told me about.

Climbing a tree, I soon saw that Friday was right. The Spaniard lay upon the beach, his hands and feet tied.

Friday and I began cautiously to advance upon the shore. But as we did so, several of the cannibals left their fire and ran towards the Spaniard. In a moment he would be killed. We could delay no longer.

Friday and I ran from the wood, firing. The cannibals fell before us, some dead, some wounded. While Friday covered me with his guns, I hurried over to the Spaniard, cut his bonds and pressed the rum bottle to his lips. He tried to speak, but I interrupted. *'Señor,'* I said in as much Spanish as I could muster, 'we will talk afterwards; but we must fight now. If you have any strength left, take this pistol and sword, and attack!'

Then the Indians were upon us again. Friday held them off as long as he could, and while I was reloading, the Spaniard plunged into battle. I saw him fighting one of the Indians with the sword I had given him. The battle was a fierce one, and as I watched I saw the Spaniard fall. I thought he must surely be killed, but at the last moment he drew his pistol and shot his attacker dead.

Of the twenty-one cannibals on the beach, only four escaped in a canoe.

Then I discovered another Indian lying in the bottom of one of the canoes. He was bound hand and foot.

I immediately cut him free, but he couldn't stand or speak. Clearly, he believed he was about to be killed by yet another enemy. I gave him a dram of rum and he was able to sit up.

When Friday looked him in the face, to his amazement he realized he was gazing at his own beloved father.

63

Friday kissed and hugged him, crying, laughing, jumping about, dancing, singing and then crying again. Later, he went to sit down beside his father and held his head. It was a deeply moving sight.

That night we all four dined together from a yearling goat. Friday was the interpreter. After so many years alone, here I was surrounded by three companions. It was unbelievable.

After dinner, I asked Friday if he would take one of the canoes, pick up the weapons we had left on the field of battle and bury the dead on the beach, as he had done when we first met. I also asked him to bury the remains of that awful cannibal feast.

May 17th, 1686

During this last month I have talked in some detail with Friday's father. He believes we have little to fear from the Indians who got away in the canoes: he is sure they will tell the rest of the tribe that they have been attacked by men who could dart fire and speak thunder and kill at a distance without lifting a hand. Only heavenly spirits or devils are thought to be able to use this kind of magic, so the tribe is unlikely to return to our shores again.

The Spaniard, meanwhile, has offered the possibility of an escape, provided I can trust his shipmates.

He told me his ship had been bound for Havana with a cargo of silver and hides. When they were wrecked, the Spanish survivors found their weapons and ammunition had been ruined by seawater. As a result, they were defenceless when they arrived on the cannibal coast.

They had managed to hold off the cannibals with their bare hands – but they had no tools, and their discussions about escape always ended in tears and despair.

When I heard this, I made a proposal. With my tools, and with the experience I had gained and passed on to Friday, we could help the Spaniards build a ship that would at last give us all the chance of setting sail for the European colonies.

The Spaniard replied that he and Friday's father would borrow one of our canoes, paddle back to their island and put the proposal to the stranded crew. He would then return with a decision.

October 10th, 1686

Today the time came for the Spaniard and Friday's father to leave. I gave each of them a musket with a flintlock and eight charges of powder and ball. I also gave them bread and raisins for the voyage.

Before they went, we all four cleared and dug more land, eventually sowing twenty-two bushels of barley and sixteen jars of rice. The harvest promises to be a good one. We will need it, if we are to make the long voyage back to the European colonies in America.

October 18th, 1686

As Friday and I waited for his father and the Spaniard to return, an unexpected incident occurred.

Friday came running up from the beach shouting, 'They are come! They are come!'

Amazed, I ran towards the shore, so eager that I didn't take any weapons as I normally would have done.

A boat was visible about a league and a half away, heading for the shore. Immediately I knew this couldn't be the Spaniard and Friday's father. We had some very different visitors, who might prove hostile.

Running back to the camp I grabbed my perspective glass and headed for the hill. From there I could clearly see a ship lying at anchor about two and a half leagues out to sea. An *English* ship, and the craft heading towards the beach was an English longboat.

Immediately my heart began to pound. I felt both joy and confusion, for why should an English ship be in this part of the world? What business could she possibly have in this wilderness?

When the boat landed I could see there were eleven men in all. Then I saw, with a chill of fear, that three of the men were unarmed and tightly bound.

Friday immediately asked if the newcomers were going to eat their prisoners.

'No,' I whispered, 'but they may murder them. I think we are watching the results of a mutiny.'

Two of the men appeared to be drunk; they stayed with the boat, and soon fell asleep.

The three prisoners waited on the sand, while the rest of their captors began to explore the beach. They did not appear to notice that the tide was going out, stranding the heavy longboat in soft sand.

After a while, the men wandered up towards the trees where they sat drinking rum for a while and then, at last, lay down and slept.

Whatever the dangers, I knew I had to contact the prisoners. Taking my weapons and leaving Friday to cover my every move, I crept up to them and asked where they had come from.

They seemed amazed. 'Are you a man or an angel, coming to rescue us?' one asked.

I looked down at my rough goatskin clothes. 'An angel would have come better dressed,' I told them ruefully.

While the mutineers slept their drunken sleep, one of the men told me the story of their plight. He said he was the captain of a ship whose men had mutinied against him; he, his first mate and a passenger were to be castaways on this desolate shore.

'Are the mutineers armed?' I asked.

He replied they only had two guns, one of which they had left in the boat. He added, 'They are led by a pair of villains – but some of the men have simply been led astray.'

As we spoke I suddenly had an idea. I told the captain that Friday and I would rescue him on two conditions. The first was that he had to obey me at all times. The second was that if we managed to recover his ship from the mutineers, the captain would take me back to England on a free passage.

The captain agreed at once.

I was overjoyed, hardly able to believe in my good fortune. This was a much better chance of escape than

building a ship with the Spaniards and risking being attacked by the cannibals.

So we set to work on the plan that was already forming in my mind. I gave the captain, his mate and their passenger three muskets with powder and ball. When the mutineers awoke, they found themselves prisoners at gunpoint.

Little wonder they surrendered, swearing to obey the captain and help take the ship from the remaining mutineers.

The captain felt that two of the men could be trusted; the others I sent under guard to my cave, warning them that if they tried to escape they would be shot.

But our task was not over yet. There were still twenty-six men on board who wouldn't give up so easily – particularly as they risked being hanged on their return to England.

Friday and the mate ran to the longboat to remove her oars and knock a hole in the bottom. Then we settled down to wait.

Hours passed.

At last the ship, still at anchor, began to fire her guns, presumably as a signal for the landing party to return.

Eventually, when none of the signalling and firing bore any result, another longboat was lowered and began to head for the shore. Soon we had a full view of the next group of mutineers.

There were ten men on the boat. The captain recognized them at once. 'Three are honest fellows,' he whispered to me. 'I'm sure they have been forced into mutiny. But the boatswain is a hardened villain, and so are his companions.'

We watched as the mutineers who had just arrived in the second longboat discovered that the bottom had been knocked out of the first. Uneasy about what had happened, they began to run along the shore, shouting out their shipmates' names.

The mutineers then stood close together and fired off a small-arms volley which made the woods ring. The birds and wild animals screamed just as they had done on the first day of my landing, so many years ago.

There was no reply to their signal.

Unnerved by the silence and then the screaming, the mutineers became fearful – and rowed back to the ship as fast as they could.

We were all horrified at this unexpected turn of events. If the mutineers gave up their companions for lost and sailed the ship away, we would all be stranded.

Suddenly the longboat swung round and was rowed back to the island again.

This time, seven men came ashore and began to search. The remaining three crew rowed the boat offshore, put down the anchor and waited.

How could we capture the seven men on the shore without alarming the three in the boat?

Just then I had an idea. I asked Friday and the ship's mate to walk over to the creek without being seen, stand on rising ground and shout 'hello' as loudly as they could.

When they heard the cries, the seven mutineers ran along the shore towards the shouting – until they came to the creek. It was high tide and they were unable to cross it – so they then called for the longboat to be brought up, just as I had hoped.

Soon the longboat reached the harbour that Friday had dug and the mutineers got out. They left two men on guard, and ran up the shore with their companions, following the shouting voices. Again they had played into my hands.

Once the crew were out of sight, we ran for the longboat, overcame the guards, and hid the prisoners in the trees.

Meanwhile, Friday and the mate were acting as decoys, drawing the men from one hill to another with their cries. They kept this going until the mutineers were exhausted. Then they made their way back to us.

When the mutineers returned, night had fallen, the tide had gone out again, and the longboat was fast aground. Immediately they flew into a panic. They were sure they had arrived on an enchanted island where they had been tormented by spirits and devils. Their panic gave us our chance: we ambushed them in the dark, and in the battle which followed, their leader, the boatswain, was shot dead. The rest of the mutineers scattered.

I asked one of the prisoners to shout into the night and to advise surrender.

'Who must we surrender to?' shouted back one of the mutineers, a man named Tom Smith. No doubt he was still thinking that he was up against the enchantment of the island.

'Your captain,' came the reply. 'He has fifty men who have been hunting you these last two hours. The boatswain is killed, and I am a prisoner. If you do not yield, we are all lost.'

So the mutineers laid down their weapons and were taken prisoner by my great army of eight. But we never let them know we were so few in number. In fact the captain told the mutineers the island had an English governor (myself!) and they were to lay down their weapons and trust to the governor's mercy!

Our next job was to repair the original longboat and work out how we were going to seize the ship from the mutineers who remained on board.

Meanwhile, the captain continued to lecture the former mutineers, assuring them that they would end up on the gallows in London or even here on the governor's island. 'As for you, Atkins –' and he turned to the man who had started the mutiny – 'you will be executed tomorrow at dawn!'

In fact this was quite untrue, but it had the desired effect: Atkins fell on his knees, begging the captain to plead with the governor to show mercy and spare his life. The other mutineers followed his example.

The captain returned to me. 'What next?' he asked.

'If we are to successfully take back the ship, we must divide up the prisoners,' I told him. 'Take Atkins and two more of the worst villains and truss them up in the cave with the other prisoners. Once the real troublemakers are out of the way, we have a chance.

'Next, tell the rest of the crew that they must remain completely loyal and ensure the mutineers still aboard the ship are captured. Take only five of the most trusted men with you, leaving their companions behind as hostages. Tell them that if there is any betrayal, the hostages will be hanged on the shore. They will believe you. Friday and I will guard the prisoners and hostages while you and your raiding party take the ship.'

It all worked as planned. The captain took his raiding party in the two longboats. As they approached the ship, one of the loyal crew called some of the mutineers out on deck: 'I've picked up the men from the island,' he told them, 'but it took a long time to find them.'

In the dark, the mutineers had no idea that the captain and the first mate were aboard the boat, until it was too late.

The mutineers on deck were quickly overcome. The rest of the raiding party then swarmed on board, locking the hatches to trap the mutineers below decks.

At last the mutiny was finally over. Our plan had worked and the ship was secured. The captain ordered seven guns to be fired. When I heard the signal, I knew the raiding party had been successful.

Exhausted, I lay down and slept soundly on the shore – until the sound of a gun made me start up, alarmed. Then I heard a voice calling, 'Governor, governor,' and I saw the captain climbing the hill towards me.

He pointed to his ship riding peacefully at anchor. Then he embraced me and said, 'My dear friend and deliverer, there's your ship, for she is all yours and so are we and all that belongs in her.'

I was overwhelmed. At last I could go home.

To prepare us for the voyage and to thank me for my help, the captain had brought a feast ashore, with cordials, wine, beef, pork, peas and biscuit – luxuries which I had not tasted since I was shipwrecked.

But best of all he brought me clothing so that I could be a civilized man again. I had clean shirts, neckcloths, gloves, shoes, a hat, stockings and a good suit of clothes of his own which fitted me remarkably well.

Five of the remaining mutineers who were still considered to be untrustworthy were given the choice of being left on the island or returned to England in chains. When they arrived they would be hanged. I spent a long time telling them about life on the island, and they decided to remain behind and take their chances. I left weapons and ammunition so they could protect themselves, and told them when the various crops we had planted would ripen. As they gazed at the chief mutineer hanging from the yardarm of the ship I could see they felt they had made the right decision.

Meanwhile, my devoted friend Friday said he wanted to accompany me back to Europe. I readily agreed, determined to look after and protect him as he had protected me.

December 19th, 1686

Today, Friday and I boarded the ship. Before we could cast off, two of the five men came swimming to the ship's side, begging to be taken off the island, claiming they would be murdered by the other mutineers. In the end we agreed to take them with us, on condition they worked hard and were good, quiet fellows for the rest of the voyage. Somehow I feel we shall have no trouble from them.

As I look leave of the island I carried on board some special souvenirs of my long stay, including a goatskin cap I had made, my umbrella, Poll my parrot, and the money I had taken from the wrecked ships.

So Friday and I have finally left the island. I have spent twenty-seven years, two months and nineteen days as a castaway, and I can hardly believe that, at long last, I am a free man.

June 11th, 1687

Today we arrived back in England.

The owners of the ship, hearing how I had saved the captain, ship and cargo, have given me the handsome present of almost two hundred pounds sterling.

Once again, I am to make a new start. So is Friday!

During the voyage home, Friday often talked to me about his father, and we wondered what had happened to him and the Spaniards. Now we've just heard from another sea captain that they returned to our island and started a colony with the mutineers. I'm sure they will be more than a match for any visiting cannibals!